English Grammar and Teaching Strategies

Lifeline to Literacy

D0266866

English Grammar and Teaching Strategies

Lifeline to Literacy

Joy Pollock and Elisabeth Waller

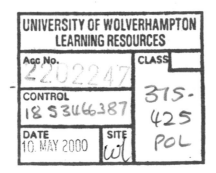

UNIVERSITY OF WOLVERHAMPTON LEARNING RESOURCES	
Acc No. 2202247	CLASS 315.
CONTROL 18 53466387	425
DATE 10. MAY 2000 SITE wl	POL

David Fulton Publishers
London

David Fulton Publishers Ltd,
Ormond House, 26–27 Boswell Street, London WC1N 3JD

First published in Great Britain by David Fulton Publishers 1999
Reprinted 1999

Note: The right of Joy Pollock and Elisabeth Waller to be identified
as the authors of this work has been asserted by them in accordance
with the Copyright, Designs and Patents Act 1988.

Copyright © Joy Pollock and Elisabeth Waller 1999

British Library Cataloguing in Publication Data
A catalogue record for this book is available from the British
Library

ISBN 1–85346–638–7

All rights reserved. No part of this publication may be reproduced,
stored in a retrieval system or transmitted, in any form, or by any
means, electronic, mechanical, photocopying, recording or
otherwise, without the prior permission of the publishers.

UNIVERSITY OF WOLVERHAMPTON
LEARNING RESOURCES

CLASS

CONTROL

DATE

Typeset by FSH Ltd, London
Printed in Great Britain by The Cromwell Press, Trowbridge, Wilts.

Contents

Acknowledgements

Our thanks go to Hilary Cook, Kate Mifflin, Karen Thompson, Val Barnes, Pete Rowe, Elizabeth Lester and many other colleagues and friends for their support and comments.

Our special thanks go to Lynda Codling for her tireless work, helpful suggestions and continual good humour while typing the script.

Introduction

About this Book

English Grammar and Teaching Strategies – Lifeline to Literacy is a practical aid for teachers, many of whom are now faced with teaching grammar without the benefit of having been taught it in their own school days. Care has been taken over the format and presentation for easy reference.

This is not a comprehensive grammar guide, but rather a practical basis on which a teacher can build. It is developed from a simple baseline and so can be used as an initial introduction, or as a form of revision as pupils move on to more complicated structures. Each year group will need to build on the information learnt in the previous years, otherwise it would be like trying to build a house without the proper foundations. Pupils in senior schools cannot progress if they have not been taught the necessary groundwork.

Each formal grammatical term is first stated succinctly and then illustrated by a variety of teaching strategies. Many of the activities suggested are for both spoken and written language, and can be used either for the whole class or small groups. It will be at a teacher's discretion to decide how much or how little of any exercise is appropriate for different levels within the class. The slower learners, children with speech and language processing problems and/or those with dyslexia will need a great deal of reinforcement in order to assimilate basic grammatical material.

The Need for Grammar

Grammar is indeed the lifeline to literacy. It is the structure of a language which we need to understand in order to be able to use that language effectively. Its correct use is essential so that people can express themselves in a way that others can understand.

One of the chief differences between people and animals is the ability to communicate fully and in many different ways. While gesture, touch, music and facial expression all play their part, our mainstay of communication is language. Different races and peoples speak different languages, but each one of these has its own conventions and structure – in other words, its own grammar. This applies equally to the spoken and written word. Inadequate and inaccurate communication skills are now commonplace. The subsequent misunderstandings may lead to problems in employment, the breakdown of friendships, and other social distress.

Although children might have their own playground language – their own code, so to speak – they also need to know and use Standard English in order for them to be properly understood in other environments. Later in their lives an employer will probably choose the candidate who impresses with well-structured language both at interview and in written application. The employee is a prospective representative of the firm and as such his or her communication skills may well be the *shop window* for the organisation.

The reason for discarding the teaching of grammar in the 1960s was, initially, to enable very small children to write freely and creatively without also having to consider points of even basic grammar. This emphasis on free expression was extended in due course to children in primary schools, and then to those at secondary school. In time, staff at universities were complaining about standards of literacy.

Languages evolve to meet the ever-changing needs of society and each generation coins new words and expressions to describe its own way of life. These changes need to be assimilated into the basic language structure, otherwise communication between generations can break down and there may be an unbridgeable gap.

It is now being recognised that a knowledge of grammar is important for each generation and that it is essential that this knowledge should be acquired in school.

It is far easier to discuss language and literature with children who know the correct terminology and therefore it is better for formal terms to be taught from the outset. However, there will be some children who may well understand the grammar but will find it hard to remember the terminology, and therefore constant revision will be essential.

English grammar is particularly complex because after the invasions of the Anglo-Saxons about AD 500, the Vikings about AD 800, and then the Normans in AD 1066, the English language that emerged in the Middle Ages had assimilated many of the grammatical structures of Anglo-Saxon, Old Norse and French. Many Latin words and conventions have come into English through French. English is now rapidly becoming the world language. People in every continent learn English as a second language and for many too it is, in fact, their first language. They learn English grammar at school. The wish of so many people to speak and write good English is resulting in our being outclassed in our own tongue.

The call now is for the return of grammar tuition so that pupils have a working knowledge of their own language. This will enable them to think clearly and express themselves effectively, as well as develop their confidence in both speaking and writing.

The Building Blocks of Grammar

Grammar may seem a daunting subject until we learn how to understand the interwoven fabric of a language. As already mentioned above, English is a composite of various languages. Consequently, it is rich and flexible, but its grammar is complex. Nevertheless, there are certain basic guidelines which help to simplify the subject.

Word order and structure of sentences are all-important. A useful analogy is that of building with Lego blocks. If the blocks are used appropriately, a well-constructed model can be achieved. Use the same blocks – or words – in a haphazard fashion and the results could be very different. Just as the blocks are dependent on their position in the model, so are words dependent on their position in the sentence to convey the meaning intended.

For instance:

I gave only George the cake.
I only gave George the cake.
I gave George the only cake.

Each of these sentences has the same words, but totally different meanings because of the position of *only*.

Children can appreciate the different functions of a word if they think of the different roles a person may fill. For instance, Paul White is a father at home, a policeman at work and a football coach on Saturday afternoons; but, he is always the same Paul White. He plays all these roles or parts.

Basically, there are eight parts of speech in English – nine if an interjection is included, which is an exclamatory remark such as *Hear! Hear!* and *Ouch!* Understanding the roles that these parts of speech play is the key to our grammar.

These eight parts of speech are:

Nouns	Verbs
Articles	Adverbs
Adjectives	Prepositions
Pronouns	Conjunctions

However, sometimes a word plays the role of one part of speech and sometimes it plays another. (See Appendix p. 87)

For instance, take the word *shout*:

I heard a *shout*.	(*shout* here is a noun)
They all *shout* together.	(*shout* here is a verb)

To decide which part of speech it is, the **whole** sentence has to be considered.

TEACHING STRATEGIES – GENERAL

Long before children are being introduced to grammatical terms they can develop a sense of language structure by playing games with words on cards. These cards can be used to introduce phonic patterns, to augment reading schemes or concentrate on particular vocabulary.

Cards can also be used to introduce parts of speech. If each of the parts of speech is represented by a particular colour, children – even at a very early level – soon recognise that there is a colour pattern indicating sentence structure. With very few words it is possible to make many different sentences.

Verbs	RED	sat, ran, hit, fell
Nouns	BLUE	man, pig, dog, hat, mum, mud
Adjectives	GREEN	red, big, fat, hot, wet, sad
Articles	BLACK	the, a

leading on to:

Pronouns	PURPLE	he, she, it
Prepositions	BROWN	on, in, at
Conjunctions	YELLOW	and

and finally:

| Adverbs | ORANGE | sadly, madly |

The above colour code is used throughout this book alongside the teaching strategy headings.

If the same colour code is used throughout the school, there is an automatic reinforcement by all teachers and a form of revision that some children find very helpful.

For instance, key vocabulary given in science:

BLUE (nouns) RED (verbs) GREEN (adjectives)

height	weigh	heavy
weight	measure	light
measurement	compare	long
length	balance	

* * * * *

Although suggestions are made for various activities throughout the book, the best teaching of grammar will often come from the children's own work. Perhaps, within the class, work on the phoneme *ck* will have led to differentiated word work. For instance, one group may have been finding words like *duck, sock, back*; others using blends for *black, stick, crack*. Others maybe adding suffixes – *quickly, kicked, packing*, or concentrating on a group such as *freckle, trickle, buckle*. Even from a word at the simplest level it is possible to build a grammar lesson, thereby including children at all levels. If each child in the class has written a short sentence, there is an instant wealth of material from which to draw.

For example, **I saw a duck**.

Where is the verb? – *saw*

What tense is the verb? – *past*

Which word is the subject? – *I*

What sort of word is *duck*? – *noun*

Can we think of words to describe a duck? – *black, white, little*

What can ducks do? – *fly, swim*

What are these *doing words* called? – *verbs*

Can we think of more information about how the ducks swim?
– *fast, quickly*

What are these words? – *adverbs*

Those told us how the duck swam – are there other kinds of adverbs that could give us more information? For instance adverbs of time – *yesterday, later, soon*

Where was the duck? – *on the farm, in the pond*

What are the little words telling us about the position of the duck? – *prepositions*

Now let's put some of this information together in some sentences:

Yesterday I saw a little black duck swim quickly across the pond.

Later the little black duck flew away.

Can we join these two sentences?

Yesterday I saw a little black duck swim quickly across the pond and later it flew away.

Can we try other ways to join the sentences?

The little black duck that I saw swim quickly across the pond flew away later.

What does the word **that** refer to in this sentence?

What happens if we change the order of the words?... and so on

At any particular stage each point can be elaborated according to the pupils being taught at that time.

A quick oral résumé provides revision for all levels within the group and ensures that those with poor literacy skills are not penalised by their slow rate of working on paper. There are always some simple questions that can be answered by those at lower stages which can then be built on by the more advanced.

Sentences

A sentence is a group of words that makes complete sense.

Over the hill leaves one wondering who or what is over the hill. It is not a sentence as it does not make sense on its own.

> The enemy is *over the hill.*
> We went *over the hill.*
> *Over the hill* flew the birds.

All these groups of words are sentences making sense on their own and are simple sentences with one main verb.

Sentences may be short or long but they must make sense.

A sentence always has a SUBJECT and a PREDICATE. In simple terms the subject is who or what the sentence is about. The predicate is what is said about the subject and must include a verb.

Subject		Predicate
Jack	–	went fishing.
He	–	went fishing for trout.
The tall thin boy	–	was fishing in the river.

In some sentences the subject does something to someone/thing. This is known as the OBJECT.

		┌─────────predicate─────────┐		
The boy (subject)	–	kicked (verb)	–	the ball. (object)
He (subject)	–	caught (verb)	–	it. (object)

A simple sentence may be:

1. A STATEMENT or declaration:

   A statement gives information. It needs a full stop at the end.

   > Emma sat by the fire.
   > He went home by bus.

2. A QUESTION:

   A question needs an answer. It needs a question mark at the end.

   > Is Emma sitting by the fire?
   > Shall we go for a walk?

3. A COMMAND or imperative:

   This is an order or request. The words spoken are written within speech marks. It often has an exclamation mark at the end.

   > "Quick march!"
   > "Sit by the fire."

4. An EXCLAMATION:

   An exclamation denotes surprise or a strong emotion. It too has an exclamation mark at the end and is written within speech marks, if being spoken.

   > "How well you look!"
   > "Well done!"

> Remember to use a capital letter after every full stop, question mark and exclamation mark.

Pupils need to be reminded that in much of their formal work a one-word answer is insufficient and they should use a full sentence:

"Are you coming?"
      not   "Yes."
        but "Yes, I am coming."
"When did William the Conqueror land?"
      not   "1066."
        but "William landed in 1066."

When we ask people a lot of questions we *interrogate* them. The word interrogate is derived from the Latin words *Rogo* – I ask and *Inter* – between.
Question sentences may be called INTERROGATIVES.

In Roman times the Imperator was a title conferred on a victorious general or emperor. These were the people who gave commands.
Commands may also be called IMPERATIVES.

In English there are three types of sentence:

1. SIMPLE SENTENCES

A simple sentence has one main verb. (This may be called a finite verb.)
The verbs are in italics.

a. Kate *climbs* mountains.
b. Tim *knows* Mark.
c. It *was living* up a tree.
d. They *are flying* to Spain.

2. COMPOUND SENTENCES

These are two (or more) simple sentences joined by a conjunction.
The conjunctions are in italics.

a. Tim knows Mark, *but* he does not know Mark's brother.
b. He sits on the river bank *and* he spends all day there.
c. James likes cake, *but* Sara has never eaten cake.
d. She does not want to eat her supper *nor* does she want to go to bed.

In a compound sentence, such as example (d), where some of the first and second parts of the sentence are repeated, one part may be omitted.

She does not want to eat her supper *nor* go to bed.

3. COMPLEX SENTENCES

Complex sentences have one main clause – which is the same as a simple sentence – and one or more subordinate clauses. Subordinate clauses are often called *embedded clauses*.

These subordinate clauses cannot stand on their own as they do not make sense unless they are attached to the main clause.

A clause is a group of words that includes a verb. (See pp. 69–71)

Examples of complex sentences with subordinate (embedded) clauses in italics:

a. The birds, *who were flying about collecting twigs*, were building their nests.

b. The van, *which was stolen*, was being followed by the police.

c. Planes usually arrive late, *when the weather is bad.*

There may be more than one subordinate clause within a complex sentence:

a. *As the sun was rising*, the explorers left their camp *in order to reach the peak before noon.*

b. *While the children waited to see the match*, their parents gathered in the hall *to hear the presentation from the headmaster.*

By listening carefully to a child's speech a teacher may be alerted to a weakness in language processing which, if ignored, can give rise to considerable difficulties in later years. Many children with such difficulties are able to communicate well with single words, incomplete sentences, the aid of facial expressions and gestures. However, they may be unable to express themselves without these props and will need plenty of practice with simple sentences before using complex sentences.

The prevalence of such problems has only been recognised comparatively recently.

Language is processed in two ways:

a. expressive language – speaking
b. receptive language – comprehending.

Some people can comprehend without difficulty, but have a problem finding words and constructing sentences in order to communicate fluently. Their grammar is often immature or weak.

Others can express themselves well but may have difficulty in comprehending what others say. These are often the pupils who fail to follow instructions properly and who need clear simple explanations.

Some people have both expressive and receptive processing problems.

Even with a reasonable knowledge of a foreign language, many of us still struggle when abroad; in the same way these pupils encounter difficulties daily in their own language.

TEACHING STRATEGIES FOR SENTENCES

These activities are all suitable for oral practice as much as for written exercises. Small groups can work together with perhaps only one member of the group being responsible for recording the answers. Most children with weak literacy skills need an enormous amount of oral work – and it is better for them to play a full part in the activity rather than struggling to write a minimal part of any exercise.

1. Ask the children to think of ten simple statements.

   They may find it helpful to have the first two words:

   a. My name ....   b. I live ....   c. I like ....
   d. My friend ....   e. Yesterday I ......   f. We play ....
   g. Dogs can ....   h. We went ....   i. They were .....
   j. The man ....

2. Ask the children to think of the questions that would have been asked, for their statements to be the answers.

3. Ask the children to think of the questions to which these might have been the answers:
   a. We went to Spain.
   b. We saw lions in the zoo.
   c. I chose it because I like the colour.
   d. Tom and his friend Bill went to London.
   e. They left at six o'clock.
   f. They used a ladder.
   g. The boys ate all the sausages.
   h. You must read the instructions.
   i. He left early to catch the train.
   j. I am going to meet my friends.

4. Ask the children to imagine they are detectives solving a crime. They must think of the questions to ask the witnesses concerning who they are, where they were and what they were doing at the time of the crime. If they work in pairs, one can ask the questions and the other reply in **full sentences**.

5. Give a mixture of phrases and sentences and ask the children to decide which are which. (See Appendix p. 88)

6. Give the children jumbled sentences and ask them to sort these into order. (See Appendix p. 89)

7. Play *Twenty Questions*. One person thinks of an object – the others must try to guess what it is by asking questions. Usually the only permitted answers are *Yes* and *No*. Try playing the game by answering the question with a full sentence:

    Is it in this room?
    No, it is not in this room.

    Is it alive?
    Yes, it is alive.

    This game can be linked to guessing characters from current reading texts or any other areas of the curriculum.

8. Imperatives

    Think of five commands given by each of the following:

    a. a general   b. a football coach   c. a teacher.
    d. a dog trainer   e. a parent

    As a written exercise this should include speech marks as well as the exclamation mark.

Nouns

There are four different kinds of nouns:

a. COMMON
A common noun is the name given to a non-specific person, place or thing:

> baby, girl, child, man, teacher, land, mountain, river, animal, bird, dinosaur, book, tree, flower.

b. PROPER
A proper noun refers to a specific person or thing, and must begin with a capital letter:

> Jack, Katy, Mrs Brown, February, Christmas, Friday, Scotland, Manchester United.

c. COLLECTIVE
A collective noun is a word used for a collection of people or things:

> organisation, crowd, navy, group, herd, flock, family, party, library, shoal, team, school.

d. ABSTRACT
An abstract noun refers to a concept, an emotion, a feeling:

> thirst, anger, happiness, consideration, freedom, ability, intelligence, thought, purpose, belief.

 It is usually possible to put the word *the* before common, collective or abstract nouns.

TEACHING STRATEGIES FOR NOUNS – Blue

COMMON NOUNS

1. Imagine an alien has landed and you wish to teach him English. An easy way would be to point to things and to name them.

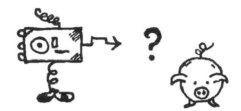

2. List 5/10/20 or as many as possible of *things* you can see in the classroom.

3. As a memory exercise, put children in pairs or small groups to play *I went to market and bought ...*

    Each player adds another item:

    a. I went to market and bought a cabbage.
    b. " " " " " " " " and a book.
    c. " " " " " " " " " " " and a cake.

This can be played using the alphabet to help pupils remember the sequence:

   apple, **b**ook, **c**ake, **d**og, **e**gg, ...

or with a single letter:

   book, **b**all, **b**un, **b**ox, **b**ear, **b**utton, **b**ean, ...

4. List categories:
   animals – wild or domestic or both
   vegetables
   furniture
   fruit
   jobs

5. Increase phonological awareness choosing five nouns of one syllable (beat) ending in a certain letter.

   d – be**d**, ro**d**, mu**d**, bu**d**, da**d**
   n – pi**n**, pa**n**, gu**n**, su**n**, ti**n.**

6. Find nouns to fit the particular spelling pattern being taught that week:

   ck – du**ck**, bri**ck**, so**ck**, sti**ck**
       – po**ck**et, ja**ck**et, bu**ck**et, ti**ck**et.

7. Find common nouns with a double letter:

   ap**p**le, ba**t**ter, ke**tt**le, fi**dd**le, bu**bb**le, cho**pp**er, ru**bb**er, wi**nn**er, pu**dd**le, sa**dd**le.

   See if the children can work out a spelling convention from their list. (The double letter follows the short vowel sounds.)

   compare: dinner – diner
             saddle – stable

> Short vowels are the initial sounds in the following words:
> **a**-pple, **e**-lephant, **i**-gloo, **o**-strich, **u**-mbrella.

PROPER NOUNS

1. Ask the children to look around the room and tell you whom they can see. Their answers should all be names. Names of people are special to them and therefore important. To show this importance we use capital letters when we write them.

   Similarly, names of countries, cities, rivers, days, months, streets, pets, and so on, are all special.

2. Can you think of a girl's or boy's name for each letter of the alphabet? (See Appendix p. 89)

3. Take your own name and think of a place to visit for each letter:
   James Smith
   Japan   Africa – Manchester – England – Sweden
   Swindon – Malaysia – Italy – Timbuktu – Hull.

4. What are the names of the characters in the book(s) you are reading?

5. Can you remember the names of the people and places in your topic work?
   Egyptians: Egypt, Nile, Vizier, Re, Amun, Horus, Isis, Anubis, Valley of the Kings, New Kingdom.

6. Use an atlas to plan a trip round the world, listing countries and/or cities.

7. List some names in the following categories:
   footballers   football clubs
   pop groups   celebrities

COLLECTIVE NOUNS

1. Sometimes we group lots of things together but give the whole group a single name. This one group is a collective noun.

How many pictures of collective nouns can pupils incorporate in one large drawing on the classroom wall?

2. Give the collective term and ask for the nouns – or give the nouns and ask for the collective term. (See Appendix p. 79)

herd   –   cows, elephants
flock   –   sheep, birds

3. Invent some new collective nouns:
a play of puppies, a bounce of boys, a giggle of girls,
a boss of grown-ups, a yumminess of sweets.

4. When all types of noun have been taught, the pupils can be divided into groups. Each group can find examples of common, proper, abstract and collective nouns.

Alternatively, a mixed list can be given, and the pupils sort them into categories of nouns.

ABSTRACT NOUNS

We can see people, places, things and collections of *things* – but there are some things we cannot see.

No, not ghosts, but abstract nouns! Abstract nouns are the *things* that could never be wrapped up in newspaper!

You would need a huge quantity of newspaper for a city, a dinosaur or a mountain – but however hard you tried you could not wrap up things like love, happiness, hunger, courage or fear!

1. Tell the story of the Greek myth – Pandora's box.

   Ask the children to list the abstract *troubles* that escaped.

2. Play the alphabet game again! Find an abstract noun for each letter of the alphabet.

3. Draw

   List appropriate abstract nouns for each.

   ☺ happiness, pleasure   ☹ misery, pain
   (See Appendix p. 90)

   Take turns to throw dice (even for ☺, odd for ☹). This will give some children more thinking time.

Singular and Plural

When we talk of one single thing we use the word SINGULAR:

one man
under a tree
on the island.

When we talk of more than one we use the word PLURAL:

some cats
under the stars.

PLURALS

1. The usual way to make a singular noun plural is to add *s*:

table	–	tables	house	–	houses
pen	–	pens	book	–	books

2. Nouns with a *hissy* sound at the end (x, s, sh, ch, z) add *es* because it makes pronunciation easier:

fox	–	foxes	waltz	–	waltzes
bus	–	buses	dish	–	dishes
watch	–	watches	boss	–	bosses

3. Nouns ending in consonant + *y*, change *y* to *i* and add *es*:

lady	–	ladies	baby	–	babies
army	–	armies	lorry	–	lorries

Nouns ending in a vowel + *y*, follow the normal rule and simply add *s*:

boy	–	boys	tray	–	trays

It is often better to give the children words that follow a rule:

donkey	–	donkeys	pony	–	ponies
tray	–	trays	lady	–	ladies
abbey	–	abbeys	city		cities
guy		guys	baby	–	babies

and to help them work out the rule for themselves, rather than simply to give the information.

4. Some nouns ending in *f* or *fe* change to *-ves* in the plural ending:

wife	–	wives	wolf	–	wolves
knife	–	knives	thief	–	thieves

Pronunciation is the best guide to those that do not change:

cliff	–	cliffs
chief	–	chiefs

5. Some nouns ending in *o* add *es*:

echoes, potatoes, heroes, tomatoes, volcanoes.

Many nouns ending in two vowels, or abbreviations or linked to music, add only *s*:

zoos, hippos, pianos, videos, cellos.

6. Some irregular plurals

mouse	–	mice	deer	–	deer
foot	–	feet	salmon	–	salmon
goose	–	geese	sheep	–	sheep
tooth	–	teeth			
child	–	children			
ox	–	oxen			
man	–	men			
woman	–	women			

Although *one* is singular, it can be used in the plural:
Are these the *ones* you want?

TEACHING STRATEGIES FOR SINGULAR and PLURAL

1. In giving pupils exercises in which singular changes to plural – or plural to singular – there are not only the nouns to consider. Pronouns, demonstrative adjectives and verbs will all be affected.

   For instance: I – we
   me – us
   he, she – they
   him, her – them
   his, her – their
   this, that – these, those
   is – are
   was – were

2. Draw five columns headed:

   s   es   ies   ves   irregular

   Ask the children to look through their reading books and find some words for each column.

3. Select a passage of text and turn all the singular words into plural and vice versa. (See Appendix p. 91)

Articles

We put *the* or *a/an* before some nouns. *The* and *A/An* are called *articles*.

    a.   definite article   –   the
    b.   indefinite article   –   a, an

        The dog – refers to a definite/specific dog.
        The dogs – refers to definite/specific dogs.

For example:

        The dog needs to be taken for a walk.
        The dogs need to be taken for a walk.

Dogs with no article – refers to dogs generally.
For example:

        Dogs need to be taken for walks.

A dog – refers to an indefinite or any dog.
For example:

        A dog needs to be taken for a walk.

If the noun begins with a vowel sound (*a e i o u*) or a silent *h*, pronunciation is made easier by inserting *n* and therefore we say:

        an aeroplane   *an* orange
        an egg   *an* umbrella
        an Indian   *an* honest man

However, in words like *unit* and *unicorn*, the initial **sound** is *y* (similar to *yes*) and therefore the article is *a* (not *an*).

TEACHING STRATEGIES FOR ARTICLES – Black

1. A simple way to give children practice, either as a class or small group activity, is to omit the articles from a piece of text and ask them to fill in the spaces. Sometimes there may be a choice.

For example:

In — morning we are going to — football match. It will be — opportunity to see — local team playing against — team from Yorkshire. Later in — day there will be — disco and — evening of fun in — old hall in — village.

2. Give a list of nouns and ask the children to choose *a* or *an* for each one. Remember to think carefully about the initial **sound** of the words:

oak bird ostrich peg girl pan chair kettle apron unicorn dress horse uncle cow oven ox yard monkey egg unit machine house aunt Italian animal table instrument apple flower engine universe

Cloze procedure, in which one part of speech is omitted throughout a text, is a useful exercise that can be used for any part of speech, and has the added advantage of encouraging discussion on synonyms.

Adjectives

An adjective is a word that describes a noun or pronoun.

In the following examples the adjectives are in italics and the nouns/pronouns which are described are underlined.

There are six kinds of adjective:

1. QUALITY – the most common kind of adjective:
   > old, big, red, wide, great, happy, hungry.
   > A *big*, *old*, *red* <u>bus</u> was driven down the *wide* <u>road</u>.

2. QUANTITY – shows how much or many are being talked about:
   > three, much, more, least, few, any, tenth, each, every.
   > *Several* <u>children</u> wanted *second* <u>helpings</u>.

3. POSSESSIVE – shows who owns or experiences something:
   > my, his, her, its, your, our, their.
   > *My* <u>brother</u> is older than *your* <u>sister</u>.

> *Its* as a possessive adjective NEVER has an apostrophe.
> (See Apostrophes, pp. 80–81)
> The dog knows *its* way home.

4. INTERROGATIVE – these are question words:

which, what, whose.
Which <u>ball</u> shall we use?

> Remember to put a question mark with question words.

5. DEMONSTRATIVE – shows or demonstrates exactly which things are talked about:

this, that, these, those.
Please put *these* <u>books</u> on *that* <u>shelf</u>.

> Interrogative and demonstrative adjectives MUST be linked to a noun. Without the noun they become pronouns.
> | | |
> |---|---|
> | *Which* <u>books</u> belong to you? | – interrogative adjective |
> | **Which** are yours? | – interrogative pronoun |
> | *This* <u>dog</u> is old. | – demonstrative adjective |
> | **This** is old. | – demonstrative pronoun |

6. PROPER – many of these are formed from proper nouns and they begin with a capital letter:

Scotland – noun	Scottish – adjective
America – noun	American – adjective

* * * * *

To compare the degree of a QUALITY between two objects we use COMPARATIVE adjectives.

This dish is hot, the other is *hotter*.

Often a comparative adjective ends in *er*:

fatter, older, wiser, nastier, happier.

Other adjectives add the word *more*:

more beautiful, *more* interesting, *more* reliable.

If there are more than two objects we use the SUPERLATIVE adjectives:

Ben is tall, David is taller but Ted is *tallest*.

Often a superlative adjective ends in *est*:

fattest, oldest, wisest, nastiest, happiest.

Other adjectives use the word *most*:

most beautiful, *most* interesting, *most* reliable.

| NEVER combine the two forms: |
| more wiser – most wisest. |

The following do not need *more* and *most*:

| good | better | best | : | bad | worse | worst |
| many | more | most | : | little | less | least |

A hyphen is used to prevent ambiguity in phrases such as:

little-used path; *well-known* footballer.

Little refers to *used* (not path); *well* refers to *known* (not footballer) and this is made clear by the hyphens.

TEACHING STRATEGIES FOR ADJECTIVES – Green

When we write or talk we are enabling the reader or listener to imagine a scene or event. The use of adjectives is essential to make the story more vivid or more exact.

1. When introducing adjectives, ask the children to close their eyes and imagine a box. Keeping their eyes shut they can change the mental image they have each time an adjective is used.

   a *huge* box
   a *pink* box
   a *pretty* box
   a *long* box
   a *battered* box
   a *leather* box

> Remember in all teaching strategies adjectives should be linked to nouns.

2. Divide the children into small groups to play *Mrs Brown's Cat.* Choose a letter of the alphabet and each child takes a turn in finding a new adjective to describe Mrs Brown's cat. The level of language/vocabulary used can vary enormously from group to group.

   Mrs Brown's cat is a *black* cat, a *brave* cat.

(See Appendix p. 92)

3. Develop listening skills by using adjectives to describe a monster. Then ask the children to draw the monster **exactly** as described:

There was a *small* monster with a *big* head. He had *three green* eyes. He had *round fluffy* ears. He had *two short* legs and *one long* one. He had a *red pointed* tail.

4. Ask the children to write or give a short description of themselves/a friend/a pet, using as many adjectives as possible:

I have *brown curly* hair.   I am *tall* and *thin*.

5. Draw a large face and ask the children to make labels to pin around the features. For example:

eyes: shiny, bright, big, blue, sparkling, sad, tearful, open
nose: snub, freckled, flat, squashy, Roman, pointed
mouth: happy, narrow, mean, smiling, wide, open, closed.

6. Give examples of *alliterations* and ask the children to invent new ones using at least three adjectives:

The *great grey-green, greasy* Limpopo river.
The *huge, heavy, hideous* hippopotamus.
A *silly, sad, slithering, slimy* slug.

7. Ask the children to find ten nouns to go with the adjective *nice*:

nice boy, nice day, nice meal, nice place.

Then ask them to keep the noun and replace *nice* with a better adjective:

friendly boy, sunny day, delicious meal, shady place.

8. Choose a prefix and see how many adjectives you can find:
   un – happy, kind, selfish, usual, sporting, likely, appealing.
   (See Appendix p. 92)

   Extend the exercise to find appropriate nouns for each adjective.

   Encourage the use of a dictionary for these exercises.

9. Choose a suffix such as *ful*, drawing attention to the single *l*:

   careful, useful, hopeful, dreadful, beautiful, pitiful, awful.
   (See Appendix p. 92)

   Similarly, appropriate nouns can be found to go with the adjectives.

Verbs

A verb is a word, or group of words, which indicates an *action* or a *state of being*. Every sentence must have a verb.

The verb is the key word in the sentence as it tells you what the subject is doing or the subject's state of being.

Many pupils think of verbs as *doing* words and extra time may need to be spent on *being* words.

ACTION – doing   Jack *runs* to school.
Diana *is combing* her hair.
The teacher *walked* into the classroom.

STATE – being   Peter *is* very tall.
Linda *has* lots of friends.
Their sister *has been* ill.

TENSES
People do not always do things NOW (in the present), but also in the past and in the future. To indicate these times verbs have TENSES. In this sense *tense* means time.

Events that have happened   – PAST TENSE
Events that are happening now   – PRESENT TENSE
Events that will happen   – FUTURE TENSE

PAST   – Yesterday he *played* football.
PRESENT – Now he *is playing* football.
FUTURE   – Tomorrow he *will play* football.

34

In many sentences two or three words make one complete verb:

He *was playing* football.
I *am playing* football.
They *will be playing* football.

* * * * *

Was, am, will be, do, is, were, shall, could, can, may, have been, are some examples of AUXILIARY verbs.

I *will be* playing: **playing** is the main verb; *will be* is the auxiliary verb.

I *can* see the fox: **see** is the main verb; *can* is the auxiliary verb.

> *Auxiliary* means helpful.
> An auxiliary nurse helps a trained nurse.
> An auxiliary teacher helps a trained teacher.

* * * * *

INFINITIVE
Verbs have an infinitive form. This tells you the name of the verb and usually has *to* before it:

to have, to sing, to run, to laugh.

Infinitive verbs are often used with auxiliary verbs (underlined):

I <u>am going</u> *to speak*.   I <u>want</u> *to come*.

* * * * *

Some *actions* or *states* occur for an instant:

Past   – I *dropped* the plate.
Present – I *drop* the plate.
Future – I *shall drop* the plate.

In other sentences the action or state continues for some time:

Past   – I *was playing* chess.
Present – I *am playing* chess.
Future – I *shall be playing* chess.

In these sentences the *playing* continues over a period of time. Therefore we use the terms:

PAST CONTINUOUS
PRESENT CONTINUOUS
FUTURE CONTINUOUS

Particularly in the early stages, the majority of children's written work is done in the past tense because they are relating or recounting past events.

For instance:

The sun *was shining* and the birds *were singing* as I *walked* down the road. Suddenly I *saw* a friend who *was riding* her bike. She *waved* to me as she *rode* by and then she *disappeared* over the hill.

> ### Bought and Brought
> *Bought* is the past tense of *buy*; *brought* is the past tense of *bring*.
>
> The two words **without r** go together;
> the two words **with r** go together.
>
> The farmer who *brought* a cow home from market might get into trouble unless he had *bought* it.

SUBJECT and VERB

Sentences have a subject and a verb. If the subject is singular, the verb must be singular. If the subject is plural, the verb must be plural. Subject and verb **must** agree.

We need to know how to conjugate (give the different forms of) a verb, so that the endings agree with the subject.

1st person singular – I	1st person plural – we
2nd person singular – you (one)	2nd person plural – you (more than one)
3rd person singular – he, she, it	3rd person plural – they

Compare the French: singular – je, tu, il/elle

plural – nous, vous, ils/elles

> Thou (sing. subj. pronoun) ⎫ Obsolete in formal
> Thee (sing. obj. pronoun) ⎬ present-day English, but
> Ye   (plural subj. pronoun) ⎭ still heard in some dialects.
>
> Ye (now You) should not be confused with Ye (meaning
> The). When Caxton brought the printing-press to this
> country from the continent in the 14th Century, there was
> no typeface for *th*. At that time this sound was represented
> in English by a y-shaped letter called *thorn*. So, he
> substituted *y* typeface for the thorn and *the* was represented
> by Ye. This can still be seen in old documents and pseudo-
> archaic names, such as Ye Olde Englishe Tea Shoppe.

As we conjugate, the forms of the verb change according to the
person and tense used:

PRESENT	PRESENT CONTINUOUS	PRESENT EMPHASIS
I play	I am playing	I do play
you play	you are playing	you do play
he/she/it plays	he/she/it is playing	he/she/it does play
we play	we are playing	we do play
you play	you are playing	you do play
they play	they are playing	they do play

He plays every day with his friend. – Present
Today they are playing very quietly. – Present Continuous
Usually they do play rather noisily. – Present Emphasis

> NEVER say *We was* or *you was* or *they was*.
> BEWARE of *I were* or *he/she/it were* (see p. 42).
> NEVER say *We does* or *you does* or *they does*.
> ALWAYS the verb must agree with the subject.

PAST	PAST CONTINUOUS	PAST EMPHASIS
I played	I was playing	I did play
you played	you were playing	you did play
he/she/it played	he/she/it was playing	he/she/it did play
we played	we were playing	we did play
you played	you were playing	you did play
they played	they were playing	they did play

He played every day with his friend. — Past
Today they were playing very quietly. — Past Continuous
Last holidays they did play rather noisily. – Past Emphasis

FUTURE	FUTURE CONTINUOUS	FUTURE EMPHASIS
I shall play	I shall be playing	I will play
you will play	you will be playing	you shall play
he/she/it will play	he/she/it will be playing	he/she/it shall play
we shall play	we shall be playing	we will play
you will play	you will be playing	you shall play
they will play	they will be playing	they shall play

Notice that traditionally *shall* and *will* in the Future and in the Future Emphasis are reversed.

Nowadays most people ignore this difference and *shall* and *will* have become interchangeable:

I *shall/will* play football tomorrow. — Future
I *shall/will* be playing football next term — Future Continuous
I *will* play football tomorrow whatever happens! – Future Emphasis

* * * * *

The subject sometimes consists of more than one word:

He and I (we) are in the garden.
Jenny and Lisa (they) were playing together.

In the case of collective nouns, confusion may arise over the correct form of the verb.

A *flock* of birds is flying over the field.
The subject *flock* is singular.
Although there are many birds, we think of them in this instance as a flock rather than individuals.

However:

The team are having their tea after the match.

This is acceptable because the team consists of individuals eating their tea. BUT – *The team is playing* refers to the team as a whole and therefore the verb is singular.

Whether the verb is singular or plural depends on how the writer considers the subject.

Agreement of indefinite pronouns with verbs may also be difficult and should be noted. (See p. 58)

ACTIVE and PASSIVE

Verbs have two forms. These are known as voices. The ACTIVE voice indicates the action the subject is taking:

The dog *bit* the man – the dog *acted.*

The PASSIVE voice shows what has happened to the subject, just as a passive person allows things to happen to him/her:

The man *was bitten* by the dog – the man was *acted upon.*

Research has shown that most children do not fully understand the passive tense until they are seven- to eight-years-old. Nevertheless, it is often to be found in early reading books.

It is explained and used in the video *Circle Time – Coming Round to Circle Time* to encourage tactful and diplomatic communication. Therefore it is better to say: "I was pushed in the playground" rather than "Tom pushed me" or "I haven't been given the book" rather than "You haven't given me the book".

PARTICIPLES

These are forms of the verb used with auxiliary verbs (see p. 35) to indicate certain tenses.

PRESENT PARTICIPLES – usually end in *ing*:
  I was *playing*.   They will be *going* home.

Present participles can also act as adjectives:
  the *shining* stars;   the *glowing* embers.

GERUNDS

A gerund is a verbal noun. It has the same form as the present participle, ending in *ing*. In the sentence "They are *smoking*", smoking is a present participle. In the sentence "*Smoking* is prohibited", *smoking* is a noun and therefore in formal writing in the sentence "Do you mind my *smoking*?" the possessive adjective *my* precedes the noun *smoking*.

Also correct: Ken's attack resulted in *his being* disqualified.

                John's playing won an award last Friday.

PAST PARTICIPLES – follow the words *has, have, had*, or *was*:
  We have *started*.   It was *forbidden*.

Many verbs which are commonly used are wrongly constructed by children who follow the normal pattern. This results for example in "we have catched", "they have bringed". Some of these common irregular participles are included in the Appendix. (See p. 94)

IMPERATIVE

The imperative form is the one word giving a command and is to be found in Direct Speech:

"Run!" "Stop!"

TRANSITIVE and INTRANSITIVE

Verbs that require an object in order for the sentence to make sense are called TRANSITIVE:

He *carried* the box
We *found* the box.

The verbs *carried* and *found* require the object (box) in order for the sentence to make sense.

Verbs that can be used without an object are known as INTRANSITIVE:

They *appeared*.
The girls *waited*.

COMPLEMENT

The verb *to be* cannot take an object but takes a COMPLEMENT:

He is a *policeman*. They were *farmers*.

Children used to be taught to say:

"It is I." "It was he/she." "It is we." "It was they."

However, nowadays we are more comfortable with:

"It's me." "It was him."

Nevertheless, it is correct to use the subject form after the verb in sentences such as:

It was *I* who did it. It was *she* who gave me the book.

CONDITIONAL VERBS

A conditional verb is used in formal writing, and often in speech too, when there is an impossible situation.

Were is used with the first and third persons singular and *would* or *should* also show the condition.

After *if*	If I *were* you...(this can never happen) ...I *shouldn't* be upset over that.
	If I *were* a mountaineer...(most unlikely!) ...I *would* climb Everest.
After *as if*	He took control as if he *were* the teacher. Ben ate as if he *were* a horse.
After *as though*	George laughed as though he *would* burst. The lion roared as though it *were* king of the jungle.

NEVER use *like* instead of *as if* or *as though* if followed by a conditional verb.

"The lion roared like it was king of the jungle."
"Ben ate like he was a horse."

BUT: it is quite acceptable to say: "Ben ate like a horse."
(See Similes p. 82)

NEVER *could of / should of / would of / might of*

This error arises from the fact that we tend to say "could've" and "should've" and *'ve* sounds the same as *of* in "I've heard *of* him."

BUT we write: I could *have* done it. You should *have* done it. He might *have* done it. She would *have* done it.

Have is part of the verb.

"I was sat there"

It is not unusual to hear such an expression these days when the intention was to explain the action *I was sitting there*.

I was sat there implies that the subject *I* has been placed there.

For instance a naughty child may be picked up and made to sit down. This would be involuntary on the child's behalf and the child might say "I was sat there until tea-time", which gives a totally different meaning from that of merely sitting there.

TEACHING STRATEGIES FOR VERBS – Red

1. Add verbs to make these into sentences.
   There may be more than one you can choose.

   a. The pig in his sty. is, sleeps, lives, was
   b. Tom the book. likes, reads, drops, wants
   c. The boy the ball. hits, kicks, sees, has, takes
   d. The dog at the cat. looks, barks, growls, snaps
   e. Ben all my toys. took, hid, lost, liked

   a. The birds on top of the roof. sang, sat, perched, gathered
   b. Cars and lorries along the motorway. raced, crept, drove, sped
   c. The explorers up the mountain. struggled, clambered, hurried, went
   d. Children some things at school. learn, write, read, notice, hate
   e. The girl by the water. hesitated, waited, stood, dawdled.

2. Ask the children to list verbs that they can do:
   I can run, I can jump, I can play, I can read.

3. Ask the children to list verbs that they cannot do:
   I cannot fly, I cannot ski, I cannot dive,
   I cannot catch an elephant, I cannot see a dinosaur,
   I cannot play a trumpet.

4a. Give a simple sentence:

The man walked along the road.

Ask the children to find alternative verbs for *walked*:

ran, went, drove, hurried, rambled, raced, strolled, trotted.
(See Appendix p. 93)

4b. The girl said, "I want to go home."

Ask the children to find alternative verbs for *said*:

stated, mumbled, muttered, cried, shouted, whispered.
(See Appendix p. 93)

5. Ask the children to take a page/paragraph or section of their reading book and change the tense from past to present or future.

6. Ask the pupils to think of an animal (noun) for each letter of the alphabet and find an appropriate verb beginning with the same letter:
the ant ambled, the bee buzzed, the camel called.
(See Appendix p. 99)

7. Most regular verbs have *ed* as the past tense ending:

stopped, hurried, played, waited, hoped, used.

Check that the pupils can use the correct word for the past tense of irregular verbs: (See Appendix p. 94)

I am (was) cold, I catch (caught) a ball, I fly (flew) a kite.

Children with speech and language processing problems will usually find these especially difficult. Even so, some may find it easier to say them aloud rather than write them. Also, using the verbs in full sentences is better than treating them in isolation.

8. Later, the same irregular verbs can be given as an exercise to find the past participle:

   I have been cold, I have caught the ball, . . .

   (See Appendix p. 94)

9. Grammar is often helpful as a spelling aid.

   For instance, the *shun* sound at the end of a noun is often *tion*. The clue may be given by the *t* sound at the end of the related verbs.

   These words are also particularly useful for practising syllable division.

Verb	Noun	Syllables
educate	education	ed – u – ca – tion
dictate	dictation	dic – ta – tion
operate	operation	op – er – a – tion

   (See Appendix p. 95)

10. Syllables are the beats in a word. To enable children to become aware of syllables, they can tap out the beats of names round the class or group.

    Tom (1 beat) Jan – et (2 beats) Jon – a – thon (3 beats)

    If a child is too tense to tap correctly, a teacher could put a hand round the child's and in this way the child begins to experience the rhythm through the teacher.

Adverbs

As its name implies, an adverb usually adds information to a verb.

Remember, every sentence must have a verb and the adverb will give the how, when and where of the action or state.

There are four categories of adverb. (In these examples adverbs are in italics and verbs are underlined.)

1. MANNER – telling how:
   He walked *slowly*.

2. TIME – telling when:
   He walked *earlier*.

3. PLACE – telling where:
   He walked *far*.

4. DEGREE – adds more information about another adverb:
   He walked *rather slowly* but she walked *very quickly*.

BUT, sometimes an adverb of degree modifies an adjective (underlined): The *very* old man told a *really* strange tale.

> Many adverbs end in *-ly*. This is called a suffix because it is fixed on to the end of a word:
>
> immediately, quickly, stupidly, happily.
>
> Make sure your adverb relates to a verb:
>
> The water <u>flowed</u> *rapidly*.
>
> BUT, the following *-ly* words are linked to a noun and are therefore adjectives:
>
> lovely day, a friendly person, a prickly hedgehog.

Adverbs, like adjectives, may be COMPARATIVE or SUPERLATIVE, but must still relate to the verbs.

COMPARATIVE ADVERBS

When comparing two actions we often use the suffix *er* or the word *more*.

(In these examples adverbs are in italics and verbs are underlined.)

He <u>ran</u> *faster* (than the others).
She <u>came</u> *earlier* (than her sister).
I <u>write</u> *more quickly* (than you).
They <u>work</u> *more carefully* (than the others).

> NEVER combine the two:
> more quicker, more cleverer.

SUPERLATIVE ADVERBS

When comparing three or more actions we often use the suffix *est* or the word *most*:

She <u>drove</u> *fastest* (of all the competitors).
He <u>arrived</u> *earliest* (of them all).
They <u>worked</u> *most carefully*.
He <u>spoke</u> *most* politely.

NEVER combine the two:
   most fastest, most earliest.

Notice the following:

badly	–	worse	–	worst
well	–	better	–	best
little	–	less	–	least

49

TEACHING STRATEGIES FOR ADVERBS – Orange

When introducing adverbs, remind pupils that it is possible to build good word pictures by describing nouns (things) using adjectives. Similarly, we can add to our word pictures by giving more information about the verbs (action words) using adverbs. They give colour and energy, intensity and vitality to a sentence.

1. Ask the pupils to close their eyes and imagine the picture for each sentence.

   Robert <u>walked</u> – the verb (action) is <u>walked</u>.

   Now HOW did Robert walk? – in what MANNER? The adverb will tell us:

   Robert walked *quickly*. Robert walked *slowly*.
   Robert walked *quietly*. Robert walked *carefully*.
   Robert walked *sleepily*. Robert walked *hopefully*.

   Similarly, using very short sentences with the same verb it is easy to demonstrate when the action happened – at what TIME? The adverb will tell us:

   Robert came *first*.   Robert came *yesterday*.
   Robert came *later*.   Robert came *tenth*.
   Robert came *next*.   Robert came *last*.

Lastly, adverbs demonstrate where – at what PLACE?

   Robert went *away*.   Robert went *backwards*.
   Robert went *far*.   Robert went *down*.
   Robert went *out*.   Robert went *back*.

DO NOT confuse adverbs of place with prepositions.
They went *down*. – adverb
They went down the road. – preposition (See p. 60)

2. Play *In the Manner of the Word*

   One pupil is given a simple sentence – for instance: "I want to go home now," – and also a list of adverbs, such as: quietly, loudly, pleadingly, angrily, gently, happily, stupidly, brightly, quickly, rudely, and so on.

   He/she must then say the sentence *in the manner of* one of those adverbs and the other pupils have to guess the adverb.

3. Choose a common verb such as *walked* and list as many adverbs as possible for *manner* and/or *time* and/or *place*:

manner	time	place
fast	first	here
slowly	earlier	outside
jauntily	later	above
hesitantly	next	about

   (See Appendix p. 96)

4. Play the alphabet game, finding an adverb for each letter:

   arrogantly, brightly, correctly, dramatically, easily ...
   (See Appendix p. 99)

5. When using adverbs that end in the suffix *-ly*, it is useful to teach pupils as a spelling guide to add the *ly* to a whole word.

   Therefore: late + ly, nice + ly, safe + ly, immediate + ly, fortunate + ly, careful + ly, beautiful + ly, awful + ly

   except words ending *le* which change to *ly*: probab~~le~~ ly, reliab~~le~~ ly, sensib~~le~~ ly, audib~~le~~ ly, possib~~le~~ ly.

6. Draw a grid with three columns – headed Noun, Adjective, Adverb:

Noun	Adjective	Adverb
faith	faithful	faithfully
beauty	beautiful	beautifully
		(See Appendix p. 97)

See how many other related words can be found.

Pronouns

A pronoun means *instead of a noun* and is used to avoid constant repetition of a noun.

For instance: Tom likes cake. Tom eats cake for tea every day with Jan. Jan gives biscuits to Will and Sam because Will and Sam like biscuits very much.

Repetition is avoided: Tom likes cake. *He* eats *it* for tea every day with Jan. *She* gives biscuits to Will and Sam because *they* like *them* very much.

Some pronouns are *instead of ONE noun* (person or thing) and are singular: I, you, he, she, it, me, him, her.

Some pronouns are *instead of MORE than one noun* (person or thing) and are plural: we, they, us, you, them.

There are different types of pronouns which may be introduced gradually as literacy levels increase:

1. PERSONAL
   These may be SUBJECT personal pronouns,
   (Remember the subject is who or what the sentence is about,)
     I, you (singular), he, she, it,
     we, you (plural), they;

or OBJECT personal pronouns,
(Remember the object is whatever is governed by the verb)

me, you (singular) him, her, it
us, you (plural) them.

NOTE needs to be made of the correct use of these pronouns.

We say "I go for a walk." – *I* is the *subject*.
We say "Richard goes for a walk."
Therefore, "Richard and *I* go for a walk."
NOT: "Richard and me go for a walk."

Similarly, "James takes me for a walk." – *me* is the object.
NOT: "James takes I for a walk."
Therefore, "James takes Ann and *me* for a walk."

ALSO: "She gave it to Will and *me*."
NOT: "She gave it to Will and I."

The same applies to plural pronouns:

We go for a walk with Richard.   – subject
Richard goes for a walk with *us*.   – object

* * * * *

IF IN DOUBT whether *I* or *me* should be used, take away the other name and it becomes clear:

Kate took Jessica and *me* for a swim.
Nick and *I* went for a pizza.

It is polite to put the other person's name before your own.

ALWAYS: Between you and me
NEVER: Between you and I

2. POSSESSIVE

Possessive pronouns show something belongs to someone:

It's *his*!
No it's not – it's *hers*!
I thought it was *mine*.
Can it be *yours*?
They thought it was *theirs* and we thought it was *ours*.
Well it must belong to someone!

> No apostrophe is used with possessive pronouns.
> Its den is in the wood. (See Apostrophes, p. 80)

3. RELATIVE

Relative pronouns relate one part of a sentence to another and should go as near as possible to the word to which they relate:

that, which, who, whom, whose, what.

They are the cards *which* I chose yesterday.
I saw the car *that* had been smashed.
See the woman *who* has lost her wig!

> The relative pronoun *that* must not be replaced by *what*.
> USE: "Those are the flowers that I picked."
> NEVER: "Those flowers are what I picked."

WHO / WHOM

Who is used as the subject and *whom* the object, which is still used in formal writing.

We caught the man *whom* we had been chasing.

We (subject) caught *him* (object). *We* (subject) had been chasing *him* (object).

Whom relates to *him*.

BUT: We searched for the man *who* was missing.

Who is the subject of the verb *was missing*.

In informal writing there is a tendency to use *who* for both subject and object.

55

4. INTERROGATIVE

Interrogative pronouns ask a question:

who, whose, which, what, when, whom?

a. *Who* did that?
b. *Whose* are these books?
c. *Which* of you can play tiddlywinks?
d. *What* did you say?
e. *When* did you cross that river?
f. To *whom* did you give the money?

Whom is little used nowadays except in formal writing.

> DO NOT confuse the interrogative pronoun *whose* with the abbreviation for *who is*
>
> *Whose* book is this? – pronoun
> *Who's* (who is) coming to dinner?

5. DEMONSTRATIVE

Demonstrative pronouns are used to specify:

this, that, these, those.

This is old; *that* is new.   (singular)
These are old; *those* are new.   (plural)

> DO NOT confuse a demonstrative pronoun (instead of a noun) with a demonstrative adjective (describing a noun).
>
> *This* is old.   – demonstrative pronoun
> *This* jacket is old. – demonstrative adjective
>   (describing *jacket*)

6. REFLEXIVE

Reflexive pronouns:

a. refer back to subject, and

b. are used for emphasis:

myself, yourself, himself, herself, itself – singular;
ourselves, yourselves, themselves   – plural.

a. He made it *himself*.

a. She helped *herself* to ice-cream.

a. You must look after *yourselves*.

b. I *myself* feel strongly about politics.

b. She *herself* sailed the boat.

b. Do you do it *yourself?*

Themselves is the reflexive pronoun.
NEVER: *theirselves*

Myself should **not** be used as a personal pronoun:

NEVER: Lucy took Harry and myself fishing.
        Myself and Kim watched a video.

BUT: Lucy took Harry and me fishing.
        Kim and I watched a video.

7. RECIPROCAL

Reciprocal pronouns express a mutual relationship:
each other, one another.

They called to *each other*. They found *one another*.

8. INDEFINITE

Indefinite pronouns are used to generalise:

a. each, any, anyone, everyone, no-one, someone, some, anything, something.

   All these are singular and therefore take a singular verb (underlined):

   Someone <u>is</u> coming. <u>Is</u> *anybody* there?
   Each of those children <u>has</u> that book.

b. many, few, several, both

   All these are plural and take a plural verb:

   Both of you <u>are</u> speaking at once.
   Many <u>are</u> called, but *few* <u>are</u> chosen.

c. neither ... nor, either ... or

   If both subjects are singular the verb is singular.
   If one or both subjects are plural, the verb is plural.

   Either the cat *or* dog <u>is</u> in the kitchen.
   Neither the cat *nor* the dogs <u>are</u> in the kitchen.

TEACHING STRATEGIES FOR PRONOUNS – Purple

1. The greatest difficulty with personal pronouns seems to be deciding whether or not the pronoun should be used in subject or object form. Should it be:

   My brother and *I* left early.
   or   My brother and *me* left early.

   (See Appendix p. 100)

2. Agreement of subject and verb is particularly difficult for some children, as the wrong usage has become commonplace in speech. For instance, should it be:

   One of the horses was lame.
   or   *One* of the horses were lame.

   (See Appendix p. 98)

3. From the text of a child's current reading book pick out the pronouns. Sort them into groups according to whether they are subjects or objects.

Prepositions

Prepositions show the *position* of nouns or pronouns (things/people) in relation to another part of the sentence.

The word preposition means *placed before* and therefore a preposition is generally placed before a noun or pronoun.

Prepositions refer to place or time.

In these examples the preposition is in italics and the noun/pronoun is underlined:

place: Edward threw the ball *over* the <u>house</u>.
The ball was *underneath* a <u>tree</u>.
The ball was *below* <u>it</u>.

time: They arrived *at* <u>midnight</u>.
I haven't been out *since* <u>Friday</u>.

Prepositions are often small words:

on, up, under, beside, across, between, about.

Some prepositions, though, are made up of groups of words:

on top of, out of, as far as, except for, in spite of.

> It is easy to confuse prepositions with some adverbs.
>
> He walked *down* the road. – preposition (relating *he* to
> *road*)
> He walked *down*.　　　　– adverb (where he walked)
> (See p. 51)

It is usual for certain words to be followed by particular prepositions:

similar *to* .... familiar *with* .... accomplished *in* ....
differ *from* .... dependent *on* .... independent *of* ....
bored *with* .... tolerant *of* .... conducive *to* ....

"off of"

There is a tendency to use both together which is incorrect.

I got it *off of* the teacher.
from is better – I got it from the teacher.

I took it *off of* him.
I took it *off* him is correct – *of* is superfluous.

TEACHING STRATEGIES FOR PREPOSITIONS – Brown

Some dyslexic students of any age may find the meanings of many prepositions difficult to grasp. For instance, they often confuse the meanings of *before* and *after*; if the teacher refers to "the word before ..." or "the letter after ...", they are lost.

1. A useful introduction to prepositions is to draw a huge mountain and ask the children to think of how many words they can relate to the mountain.

   They could also make a plasticine model.

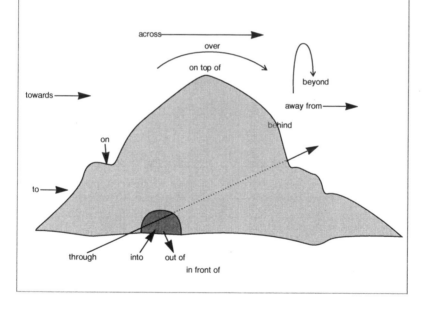

2. Ask the children to give directions for a treasure hunt including as many prepositions as possible:

Go *down* the hill. Walk *across* the bridge to the forest. Walk *through* the forest, *under* the trees *beside* the stream and *round* the lake ...

3. Physical activity with the children actually moving *beside* the chair, *under* the table, *near* the door, and so on, is particularly good for those with poor spatial concepts.

4. Children can be given instructions such as:

Jack stand *behind* Pat. Ken stand *between* Susie and Zoe. Rob go *in front of* Ken but *behind* Louisa ...

The number of instructions may be lengthened or shortened according to the listening span of the children concerned.

Conjunctions

In the same way as a road junction connects roads going to various places, so a conjunction connects sentences or clauses. There is a signpost at a road junction. A conjunction is similar to a signpost. The listener or reader needs to understand the *signpost* or the meaning will be lost.

CO-ORDINATING CONJUNCTIONS connect words, phrases, sentences. The most used are *and, but, or*. Others are *then, yet, either ... or, neither ... nor*.

   a. words   bread *and* butter
   b. phrases   in sickness *or* in health
   c. sentences He had a map with him, *but* he still got lost.

When two equal sentences are joined by a conjunction, they become a *compound sentence*: (See p. 11)

They went to visit the zoo *and* they saw the penguins.

A conjunction that connects a simple sentence with further information is known as a SUBORDINATING CONJUNCTION. (See pp. 70–71)

   a. He went on the swings *although* it was time to go to bed.
   b. Janet ran away *because* her brother was singing.

Examples of subordinating conjunctions are:

when, where, because, after, if, that, until, however, unless.

Some have more than one word:

in order that, as long as, in case.

TEACHING STRATEGIES FOR CONJUNCTIONS – Yellow

1. Make up sentences using conjunctions:

   although, while, also, until, unless, whether, after, as, that, since, because, before.

2. Give the sentences without the conjunctions and ask the pupils to suggest suitable ones:

   Although she missed the bus she was not late.
   You must stand still *while* you are waiting.
   She was told *where* to put her coat.
   Wait here *until* I am ready.
   Do not come *unless* you would like to.
   He wanted to know *if/whether* it were possible.
   They went out *when/after* they had eaten their lunch.
   As we may be late, please do not wait.
   He would play football *as long as* it was light.
   We have not been out *since* it stopped raining.

3. Give the following conjunctions:

   so, as, after, when, because, before.

   Then write each of the sentences (a) to (e) in at least five different ways.

   a. We finished our work and then left the house.

   We left the house *because* we had finished our work.
   When we had finished our work we left the house.
   We had finished our work *so we* left the house.
   As our work was finished we left the house.
   We left the house *after* the work was finished.

   b. The boys had lost the dog and they were upset.

   c. He broke the vase and then he mended it.

d. She had a cup of tea and then fed the cat.

e. He played football before dinner.

4. Ask the children to see how few sentences they can use to give the following information without using the words *and* or *then* more than once. The order may be varied.

    I woke up.
    I dressed.
    I had breakfast.
    I went to school.
    I wrote a story.
    I played football at break.
    I read my book.
    I had fish and chips for lunch.
    I went swimming.
    I watched television.
    I cleaned my teeth.
    I went to bed.

5. The examples of adverbial clauses on pages 70 and 71 can be used to show children how to join sentences effectively.

The meanings of conjunctions are difficult to grasp for many people – especially those who have a speech and language processing problem or who are dyslexic.

Phrases

A phrase is a group of words which does not contain a verb and does not make sense on its own. Therefore it is not a sentence. There are different kinds of phrases.

1. ADVERBIAL PHRASES

     These tell us the *how, when* and *where.*
     In the following examples the adverbial phrase is in italics and is linked to the verb which is underlined:

     The soldiers <u>marched</u> *as fast as possible.*   – how
     The soldiers <u>marched</u> *in the early morning.* – when
     The soldiers <u>marched</u> *far over the hills.*   – where

2. ADJECTIVAL PHRASES

     These tell us more about the nouns or pronouns in a sentence.

     The phrase in italics is linked to the noun/pronoun which is underlined:

     The <u>soldiers</u> marched *in full battle gear.*
     <u>They</u> marched *in full battle gear.*

3. NOUN PHRASES

     These act as nouns.

     The phrase in italics in the following example is the subject:

     The girl with auburn hair has good dress sense.

4. PREPOSITIONAL PHRASES

These phrases give the position of the nouns/pronouns:

<u>The trees</u> *at the bottom of the garden* are very old.

Clauses

A clause is a group of words which includes a verb.

MAIN clauses make sense on their own and are similar to simple sentences.

SUBORDINATE clauses (embedded clauses) add information to the main sentence and are therefore classified according to their functions: noun, adjectival, adverbial. They cannot stand as a sentence on their own.

1. NOUN CLAUSES

   These can be replaced by a <u>noun phrase</u>:

   a. I shall always remember *that you have helped me*.
      I shall always remember <u>your help</u>.

   b. He knows *what he should do*.
      He knows <u>his duty</u>.

2. ADJECTIVAL CLAUSES

   These often begin with *who, that, which, whom*. They can be replaced by an adjective describing a noun in the main clause:

   a. The hat, *which is a lovely blue*, suits her very well.
      The <u>lovely blue hat</u> suits her very well.

   b. The duck swam across the pond *that is in the village*.
      The duck swam across the <u>village pond</u>.

   c. The woman visited her mother *who was sick*.
      The woman visited her <u>sick mother</u>.

3. ADVERBIAL CLAUSES

These are the most widely used clauses and they do the work of an adverb. They tell us *how*, *when*, *where* and *why*. There are eight types of adverbial clause.

Detailed analysis is unlikely to be necessary at primary level, but types of adverbial clause are listed below to facilitate recognition:

a. Clauses of Time

   I will tell you *when you sit down.*

b. Clauses of Place

   We played in the wood *where the bluebells grow.*

c. Clauses of Condition

   He will help you *if you ask him politely.*

d. Clauses of Reason

   They went to Switzerland *because they love mountains.*

e. Clauses of Manner

   The children worked *as hard as they could.*

f. Clauses of Purpose

   The prisoner was punished *so that he would never steal again.*

g. Clauses of Concession

   Although he was small he could run very fast.

h. Clauses of Comparison

   These boys sang *as well as the boys in the choir.*

> Clauses function in various ways and these depend on the context in which they are used. It is necessary to consider the **whole** sentence.

The misplacing of clauses, phrases or even words within sentences can give a whole new meaning to the one intended.

For instance:

I want my hair cut badly.

At St Trinian's school, tickets for the function on Saturday cost £5.00 including wine and nibbles from the Head.

She kept a picture of them on the beach.

He saw the new statue crossing the road.

Did you see the clock going upstairs?

I saw the football team played well in the newspaper.

The family left Africa where they had spent three years in a plane.

The man bought the stool from the lady with a padded seat.

Speech

DIRECT and INDIRECT

Direct speech is what someone says. The actual words spoken are indicated by speech marks/quotation marks:

"We had lots of fun at the party," said Lauren.

Speech marks are not used in Indirect or Reported Speech because they are not the **actual** words said:

Lauren told her mother that the party had been fun.

SPEECH MARKS

Speech marks are used to indicate to the reader the actual words that someone says. Any related punctuation goes within the speech marks:

"We'll go to the seaside tomorrow," Janet said.
"Try not to be late!" pleaded William.
"Are you going away next half-term?" asked Sam.

A comma may precede the words within the speech marks:

Julie said, "I am leaving after dinner."
"Stay for a while," she said, "we need your help."
Jack exclaimed, "What a fantastic meal!"

To clarify conversations for the reader it is important to use a new line for each speaker. If one speaker continues and paragraphs are needed, speech marks are used at the beginning of each paragraph, but not closed until the end of the last paragraph when that speaker has finished.

When changing direct into indirect speech, the tenses of the verbs that were within the speech marks change:

For instance: "I'm winning!" he shouted.

He shouted that he *was winning*.

"I am going to play," she insisted.
She insisted that she *was going to play*.

Any words denoting exact time may also change:

today   – that day
yesterday – the day before, the previous day
tomorrow – the next day, the following day
now   – then, at that time.

For instance:

She said, "I will do it now."
becomes: She said that she would do it then.

She said, "I will do it tomorrow."
becomes: She said she would do it the next day.

TEACHING STRATEGIES FOR
DIRECT and INDIRECT SPEECH

Many children are familiar with comics and cartoon strips that use speech bubbles. These are a useful aid in teaching direct speech because the children can see that the words contained in the bubble are the exact words coming from the character's mouth. Similarly, only the exact words spoken are contained in speech marks. The speech marks replace the speech bubbles in written work, regardless of their position in the sentence.

Fat Sam said, "Have you seen my dog?"
Slim Jim replied, "Not since yesterday."
or
"Have you seen my dog?" asked Fat Sam.
"Not since yesterday," answered Slim Jim.

For greater emphasis children could write the words within the speech marks in a different colour.

1. a. Ask two children to role play for a short conversation. For instance, one goes to a shop to buy some sweets; the second is the shopkeeper.

   b. Then ask the children to write down what has happened in indirect speech.

      Jo went into the shop and asked the man for some sweets. The man wanted to know what sort ...

   This exercise is also useful to show how confusing a piece of work may become with overuse of the pronoun *he*.

   For instance:

      Jo went into the shop and asked the man for some sweets. He said to him that he wanted to know what sort and he was not sure so he asked him to show him what he had.

2. a. Ask one child to interview another, perhaps on a topical subject.

   b. Then each pretends to be a newspaper reporter and writes an account of the interview.

Punctuation

Children sometimes fail to realise that the need to punctuate is for the benefit of their readers and is not merely an exercise set by the teacher. Punctuation enables the reader to interpret exactly what the writer is trying to say.

The capital letter at the beginning of a sentence and the full stop at the end indicate the words that go together and make complete sense. Suggest children read from the middle of one sentence straight through the full stop to the middle of the next. They will then realise the need for a full stop. By reading their work aloud they appreciate the necessity to pause for breath. Also, it is easier for them to see if their written work makes sense.

Both a question mark at the end of a question sentence and an exclamation mark after an exclamation already include a full stop.

 For those who often reverse the ?, remind them that the curve is swallowing the words of the question:

Do you want a biscuit

COMMAS

The comma separates words (especially in a list), phrases and some clauses. It is not used as often as it used to be and, providing the meaning is clear, is considered to be superfluous. The flow of the sentence may be improved.

However, in other cases, commas may be essential to clarify the meaning and to indicate how the sentence should be read.

For instance compare:

If we decided not to swim then, Mandy and Ann would be pleased. *Then* is linked to *swim*.

If we decided not to swim, then Mandy and Ann would be pleased. *Then* is linked to *Mandy* and *Ann*.

Commas separate elements that are not part of the main sentence:

It seems, *however*, that this is not yours.
It was, *nevertheless*, the best thing to do.

1. COMMAS separate words:

On the floor of Dan's bedroom were his socks, football boots, a sticky bun, three blocks of Lego, a hairbrush and a mug.

There is no need for a comma between the last two items of a list which are joined by *and*.

However, note the following:

Zoe went to Boots, W.H. Smith, Sainsbury's, and Marks and Spencers.

The comma before *and* shows that Marks and Spencers go together and means one shop.

When two adjectives are often used together there is no need for commas:

deep blue sea; poor old thing.

2. COMMAS separate phrases:

> Between you and me, I don't understand any of it!
>
> Down the lane, past the shop, over the bridge, and there you will see the old house.

3. COMMAS separate clauses:

> It was a bright and sunny day, but in the evening there was a thunderstorm.

4. A COMMA may be needed to prevent momentary confusion:

> With the dog chasing, the cat fled across the garden.

SEMICOLONS

Semicolons are very useful for joining phrases/clauses and sentences. They are effective when a full stop would be too disjointed, and a comma too weak. They can improve a writer's style, enabling a piece of writing to have more impact.

> You should always try to be pleasant; never lose your temper.
>
> Drive as carefully as possible; though not too slowly.
>
> You should take some exercise every day; this should be done first thing in the morning.

In these sentences, commas would be insufficient and full stops would weaken the adherence of the first and second parts.

COLONS

A colon is used to introduce a list. It is NOT followed by a capital letter:

> The school needs the following items before next term: exercise books, reading books, stationery, games equipment.

It is also sometimes used to make a greater emphasis than the semicolon when joining clauses and sentences:

> There is something you should know: that man is a spy.

Paragraphs

Paragraphs are used to divide up a piece of writing. Each paragraph should make a particular point when an essay or a report is being written. In a story it is usual to use a new paragraph when introducing a new person, place, change of time, or new event.

Each new paragraph begins on a new line. In writing down speech, each time the speaker changes there is a new paragraph and therefore a new line.

Many reports require an introduction in the first paragraph. This is followed by a new paragraph for each new point. The final paragraph is used to summarise or draw a conclusion.

These days, from an early stage, children are taught to plan their written work. Points to be made can be numbered for developing into paragraphs.

Apostrophes

The apostrophe is often omitted or misplaced because of uncertainty over its use. Some simple guides ensure its correct use. **However, it is inadvisable to teach both contractions and possessives at the same time, or too soon after plurals.**

CONTRACTION

An apostrophe is used to denote that one or more letters have been omitted and the word shortened.

Don't	– do n(o)t	Where's	– where (i)s
Six o'clock	– six o(f the) clock	We'll	– we (sha)ll, wi(ll)
I've	– I (ha)ve	They're	– they (a)re
He's	– he (i)s, (ha)s	Who's	– who (i)s, (ha)s

It's meaning *it is* or *it has* should not be confused with the possessive pronoun *its* – *It's* hurt *its* paw.

POSSESSION

If an object belongs to a single person or persons we add an *'s*. As the letter *s* is also added to a noun to form a plural, the apostrophe indicates ownership.

Dan has a cat. It is Dan's cat.
Jenny keeps rabbits. They are Jenny's rabbits.

If the *ownership* is plural, write the plural word, then add an apostrophe after the *s*.

The dogs' dinner – the dinner belonging to the dogs.

OR, if the plural word does not end in *s*, add apostrophe *s*.

The children's playground.
The men's club.

If the ownership word already ends in *s*, like Charles, it is traditional to add the apostrophe after the *s*:

Charles' home; James' bike.

However, one also sees Charles's home. Much depends on the pronunciation, but either is acceptable.

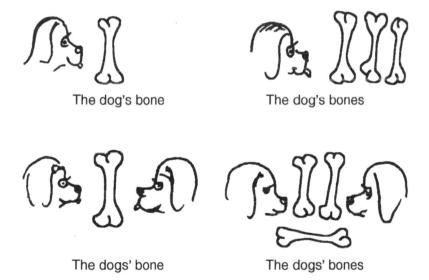

The dog's bone   The dog's bones

The dogs' bone   The dogs' bones

One's is the only possessive pronoun to have an apostrophe.

One looks to *one's* survival.
One may work for *one's* own benefit.
One should see *one's* dentist regularly.

Figures of Speech

SIMILES

A simile compares two things by saying they are *like/similar* to each other:

Tom is like a giant.
The lamb's fleece was white as snow.

METAPHORS

A metaphor compares two things by saying that one thing is the other:

Tom is a giant.
The man barked at his assistant.

ALLITERATION

Alliteration is the use of a repeated sound to create an effect:

The silence surged softly backwards.
(Walter de la Mare – The Listeners)

Round the rugged rocks the ragged rascal ran.

ONOMATOPOEIA

Onomatopoeia refers to words that imitate the sound that they describe:

cuckoo, quack, swish, splash.

Synonyms and Antonyms

SYNONYMS

Synonyms are words with almost the same meaning:

ghastly, horrible, frightful, shocking, terrible, dreadful, grim, horrendous, (adjectives);

think, consider, reflect, ponder, imagine, believe, deliberate, contemplate, (verbs).

ANTONYMS

Antonyms are words which have opposite meanings:

hot – cold, wet – dry, happy – sad, generous – mean, noisy – quiet, tense – relaxed (adjectives);

admit – deny, love – hate, live – die, increase – decrease, give – take (verbs).

When finding synonyms and antonyms, it is important to keep to the same part of speech; nouns for nouns, adjectives for adjectives, and so on.

It may be easier for some children to have the original word in the context of the sentence before attempting to find synonyms or antonyms for it.

Homonyms, Homophones and Mnemonics

HOMONYMS

Homonyms are words with the same spelling but different meanings:

rear – to raise children
rear – a horse rising on its hind legs
rear – at the back
burn – ignite
burn – Scottish stream

HOMOPHONES

Homophones are words pronounced the same, but with different spellings and meanings:

minor/miner, stationery/stationary, there/their, great/grate, birth/berth, air/heir, paw/pore/pour, born/borne, dear/deer, heard/herd, here/hear, bear/bare, rough/ruff.

MNEMONICS

A mnemonic is an aid to memory; it enables a person to recall some information. For instance, to recall the correct spelling of stationary/stationery, the following may help:

A c*ar* is station*ary*.   Pap*er* is station*ery*.

Conclusion

English, like any other language, is continuously changing. However, it is essential to understand the basic grammatical structure and to use it in order to communicate ideas and information clearly. It is important that both speaker and listener, writer and reader, are aware of this coding system called grammar.

It is hoped that this practical introduction to the subject may become the beginning of a lifetime's interest in a search for clear and succinct communication. For some it may become a fascination; for others it may always be a struggle. Whichever it is, nothing could be more worthwhile for pupils at school to learn how to use their language effectively. Without that knowledge they may be handicapped and frustrated for life.

Inevitably, in writing this book decisions had to be made over what to include and what to leave out. Sometimes the choice has been difficult, but the aim has been to lay a firm foundation from which may be gained a good working knowledge of the English language.

Appendix

Examples of Words Performing Different Functions (Page 4)

Please may I have a *drink*? (noun)
She will *drink* milk at bedtime. (verb)

The shoppers were streaming *in*. (adverb)
Put the dog *in* the kennel. (preposition)

The teacher was very *cross* with me. (adjective)
Cross out all the mistakes. (verb)

He was the *only* boy to remain after the lesson. (adjective)
You can *only* do your best! (adverb)

"Get *down* at once!" shouted the man. (adverb)
The rain trickled *down* the window pane. (preposition)

Have you seen lions in the *wild*? (noun)
The *wild* animals roared fiercely. (adjective)

Give my *love* to your mother. (noun)
He would *love* to visit Disneyworld. (verb)

That is an unusual butterfly. (pronoun)
Please give me *that* book. (adjective)

Sentences and Phrases – Three Levels of Difficulty (Page 15)

Decide which of the following are sentences and which are phrases:

a. Jam and cake for tea	ph
b. The dog ate his bone	s
c. Sweets are not good for dogs	s
d. The ship with the cat on it	ph
e. When walking in the garden	ph
f. There was once an old king	s
g. One of them is in the box	s
h. The top shelf in the kitchen	ph
i. The best of the books	ph
j. He was not at home	s

a. All the flowers in the garden	ph
b. The bears ate porridge for breakfast	s
c. Chocolate biscuits are not eaten by tigers	s
d. The aeroplane with the cat on board	ph
e. While walking over the mountains	ph
f. Once upon a time there was an old Sultan	s
g. None of them was able to reach the shelf	s
h. The highest shelf in the cupboard	ph
i. Our first in the new term	ph
j. I had a feeling of mystery and danger	s

a. Recovery from a recent serious illness	ph
b. Confidence is the key to success	s
c. Words opposite in meaning to each one below	ph
d. Having too high an opinion of oneself	ph
e. Describe, in your own words, the girl's father	s
f. A shop which sells newspapers at the end of the street	ph
g. A last glance at the moorings of the boat	ph
h. Youth is the time for adventure	s

Jumbled Sentences – Two Levels of Difficulty (Page 15)

Put the words in the order that makes sense:

a. bit the the man dog.
b. looked I the at box.
c. home with my I sister went.
d. sun likes the to he sit in.
e. at he was home not.
f. my bus stops red house at the.
g. play at football school we.
h. see him to going am I.
i. four and two two make.
j. this from cat drinks the dish.

a. river of an bank the oak the grew on tree.
b. which looked I on the at box table lay.
c. city next the walk morning took he a the in.
d. home Charlie brother with my went Tom and.
e. left the people early several concert.
f. the walk do dangerous ice on not thin.
g. books may from you five library the borrow.
h. door left up boys lined the on door the of.
i. brightly flames the fire blazed of the.
j. over lessons may you as leave soon are as.

Alphabetical Names (Page 19)

Alice Bridie Carmen Daisy Esther Fiona Gabriella Hannah Isobel Jessica Kelly Lucy Maudie Natalie Olivia Penny Queenie Rosie Susie Tamsin Una Vicky Wendy Xneia Yasmin Zoe

Adam Barry Corrin Daryl Edward Freddie Gary Harry Ian James Ken Lee Mohammed Nathan Oliver Patrick Quentin Richard Simon Tim Unwin Victor Will Xavier Yuri Zachary

Common Collective Nouns (Page 20)

herd	cows, deer		constellation	stars
flock	sheep, birds		pack	wolves, cards
army/regiment	soldiers		batch	loaves
hive/swarm	bees		flight	stairs, finches
staff	teachers		fleet	ships, cars
host	locusts		crowd	people
collection	stamps		exaltation	larks
throng	merrymakers		school	whales
gaggle	geese		mass	people
shoal	fish		bunch	grapes, flowers
band	robbers		colony	ants
pride	lions		team	players
library	books		gang	thieves, workmen
brood	chicks		litter	kittens, puppies
crew	sailors		tribe	monkeys, people

Abstract Nouns (Page 21)

☺	☹
happiness amusement beauty joy faith hope success pleasure peace wonder love wisdom sanity mirth affection courage music patience tolerance justice freedom liberty equality dream laughter ambition companionship truth	pain disease agony misery suffering fear sorrow terror hate worry anxiety despair grief shortcoming bitterness envy spite jealousy ugliness adversity thirst frustration anger despair loathing hatred evil nightmare

Singular and Plural (Page 25)

Pick out singular and plural words from the following text. The plural nouns could be put in categories according to their endings.

One day when the children were at summer camp, they decided to go for a walk. After washing up the breakfast dishes and knives and forks and making their beds, they set off down the lane. There were ten boys, eight girls, five dogs and two puppies. After walking about a mile all the dogs and puppies became very excited and the children suddenly saw that they were alongside a field where sheep were grazing. The girls became very worried in case the dogs started chasing the sheep.

Fortunately, just then some lorries passed the children and these had soldiers in them who were armed with guns and knives. The noise they made distracted the dogs and they began to chase the lorries instead.

When the dogs returned, they wagged their tails and looked like brave heroes for chasing the lorries. However, they did not like being put on their leads and having to walk with the children.

They met some girls riding their ponies, and later, three families who were clearing away dead leaves at their feet. They were trying to find their car keys which one of the wives had lost.

In the afternoon the children sat down to rest by a stream. They told each other stories while eating their sandwiches, and they pretended to see foxes and monkeys and hippos and wolves in the woods, and snakes and mice in the ditches.

At last, tired and hungry, they got back to camp. They ate a huge supper of meat, potatoes, carrots, tomatoes and beans which they cooked by themselves. Then they were glad to go to bed. Soon all of them had fallen sound asleep.

Adjectives Beginning with *b* – Mrs Brown's Cat (Page 31)

big bad black brave British broad bouncy beautiful bright blind brindle brainy brash brilliant boring blooming brown babyish blasted bedridden beaming brutal bronze bothered barmy batty bestial bewildered bewitched bewitching boisterous bubbly bumptious bucolic benign bountiful banal bereaved bigoted biddable bad-tempered

Adjectives with Prefix *un* (Page 33)

unlikely unappreciative unkind unusual unafraid unaware unabashed unabridged unfaithful unruly unsteady unpleasant untidy unsure uncertain unconnected unmistakable unknown unscientific uncooked unselfish unwary unwelcome unsympathetic

Adjectives with Suffix *ful* (Page 33)

careful useful hopeful dutiful beautiful plentiful graceful dreadful mournful sorrowful blissful doubtful pitiful awful helpful tactful thoughtful wonderful truthful deceitful fearful joyful playful

Alternatives for *walked* (Page 45)

trotted ran dawdled strolled ambled meandered marched raced
rushed dashed charged limped staggered hobbled stumbled tiptoed
danced crept slipped crashed

Alternatives for *said* (Page 45)

muttered mumbled demanded pleaded asked enquired interrupted
commanded begged ordered contradicted requested entreated
barked snapped bellowed roared yelled shouted whispered
repeated insisted complained moaned groaned stated declared
questioned persisted denied agreed confirmed alleged swore
promised

Some Common Irregular Verbs and Past Participles (Pages 40, 45 & 46)

Present	Past		Past Participle
am	was	(I have)	been
begin	began	"	begun
break	broke	"	broken
bring	brought	"	brought
buy	bought	"	bought
catch	caught	"	caught
creep	crept	"	crept
draw	drew	"	drawn
drink	drank	"	drunk
drive	drove	"	driven
eat	ate	"	eaten
fall	fell	"	fallen
find	found	"	found
fly	flew	"	flown
forget	forgot	"	forgotten
go	went	"	been
grow	grew	"	grown
hear	heard	"	heard
know	knew	"	known
leave	left	"	left
light	lit	"	lit
make	made	"	made
ring	rang	"	rung
run	ran	"	run
see	saw	"	seen
sing	sang	"	sung
sink	sank	"	sunk
sleep	slept	"	slept
swim	swam	"	swum
swing	swung	"	swung
tear	tore	"	torn
think	thought	"	thought
throw	threw	"	thrown
write	wrote	"	written

Verbs Ending in *te* and *t* with Related Nouns Ending in *tion*
(Page 46)

educate – education

eliminate – elimination

generate – generation

dominate – domination

concentrate – concentration

penetrate – penetration

illustrate – illustration

elaborate – elaboration

inject   injection

connect – connection

correct – correction

object – objection

erect – erection

operate – operation

irritate – irritation

fascinate – fascination

elevate – elevation

initiate – initiation

animate – animation

devastate – devastation

indicate – indication

inspect – inspection

collect – collection

direct – direction

reject – rejection

elect – election

Some Adverbs Linked to the Verb *walked* (Pages 50–52)

Manner	Time	Place
slowly	sooner	along
fast	later	afar
jauntily	earlier	away
quietly	next	backwards
swiftly	first	forwards
daintily	second	closely
stealthily	last	near
determinedly	then	together
abjectly	now	further
hurriedly	before	across

Connected Nouns, Adjectives and Adverbs (Page 52)

Noun	Adjective	Adverb
faith	faithful	faithfully
hope	hopeful	hopefully
beauty	beautiful	beautifully
pity	pitiful	pitifully
duty	dutiful	dutifully
peace	peaceful	peacefully
marvel	marvellous	marvellously
fame	famous	famously
glory	glorious	gloriously
victory	victorious	victoriously
nerve	nervous	nervously
danger	dangerous	dangerously
infection	infectious	infectiously
courage	courageous	courageously

Agreement of Verb to Subject (Page 39)

A regiment of soldiers *was* billeted in the town.

Each of the children *has* an apple.

Two of the boys *have* been here before.

None of the girls *has* been here before.

All the children *enjoy* the holidays.

One of the children *likes* mushrooms.

Ham, Shem and Japeth *were* in the ark.

Everyone *wants* to be chosen first.

The flock of birds *was* on the roof.

One of the twins *was* lost in the woods.

Alphabetical Parts of Speech (Pages 45 & 51)

Adjective	Noun	Verb	Adverb
aged	ant	ambled	aimlessly
big	baboon	behaved	badly
calm	cow	chewed	contentedly
dirty	dog	dribbled	dreadfully
energetic	elephants	entertained	enthusiastically
frightened	fox	fled	furtively
great	goat	gobbled	greedily
huge	hare	hopped	happily
intelligent	iguana	inspected	intently
jolly	jaguar	jumped	jauntily
kind	kangaroo	kicked	keenly
lazy	lion	laughed	loudly
minute	mouse	munched	madly
nimble	newt	nibbled	nervously
old	owl	observed	offhandedly
precious	peacock	paraded	proudly
quiet	queen	questioned	quickly
ragged	rabbit	ran	rapidly
slippery	snake	slid	silently
timid	tiger	trembled	terribly
unusual	unicorn	understood	urgently
vast	vole	vanished	violently
wicked	weasel	walked	warily
young	yak	yawned	yesterday
zany	zebra	zig-zagged	zippily

Use of *I* and *me* (Page 59)

Please keep five copies for Jan and *me*.

Both my brother and *I* enjoy football.

Would you please give the tickets to Pete and *me*?

Between you and *me*, it's a secret.

Send Louisa and *me* all the information you have.

At the end of the day it is my sister and *I* who will have to choose.

David and *I* are going to the seaside tomorrow.

Send the parcel to *me* next week, please.

Vicky and *I* are playing tennis on Saturday.

It was Sara and *I* who did it.

When will he give the book back to John and *me*?

Ken visited Bill and *me* last Monday.

It was Olive and *I* who went to the village.

He bought a drink for Kate and *me*.

It is the teacher and *I* who will play the duet.

Further Reading

Books

The Complete Plain Words by Sir Ernest Gowers. Revised by Sidney Greenbaum and Janet Whitcut. Published by Penguin Books 1987.

Usage and Abusage by Eric Partridge. Published by Penguin Books 1973.

Modern English Usage by H. W. Fowler. Published by Wordsworth Editions 1994.

Rediscover Grammar with David Crystal. Published by Longman 1988.

Who Care's about the English Language? by David Crystal. Published by Penguin 1984.

The English Language by Robert Burchfield. Published by Oxford University Press 1985.

The Cambridge Encyclopedia of the English Language by David Crystal. Published by Cambridge University Press 1997.

The Right Word at the Right Time: A Guide to the English Language and How to Use It. Published by the Reader's Digest Association 1985.

Signposts to Spelling by Joy Pollock. Published by Heinemann 1980.

Day-to-Day Dyslexia in the Classroom by Joy Pollock and Elisabeth Waller. Published by Routledge 1994.

Video

Circle Time – Coming Round to Circle Time. Bristol: Lucky Duck
  Publications.

UNIVERSITY OF WOLVERHAMPTON
LEARNING RESOURCES